Emergency Vehicles

Police Car

Chris Oxlade

QED Publishing

6244493.

Author Chris Oxlade
Project Editor Eve Marleau
Designer Susi Martin

Publisher Steve Evans
Creative Director Zeta Davies
Managing Editor Amanda Askew

Picture credits
(t=top, b=bottom, l=left, r=right, c=centre, fc=front cover)
Alamy
4l Goss images; 6–7 Paul Springett A; 7r Justin Kase zfourz; 8–9 Howard
Sayer; 10 ACE STOCK LIMITED; 11 Jack Sullivan; 12–13 fine art
Chris Taylor, with thanks to the Metropolitan Police
16–17, 17l
Corbis
9r DiMaggio/Kalish
Photolibrary
13r Thomas Frey
Shutterstock
1; 4–5 MalibuBooks; 14–15 Samuel Acosta; 15 Andresr; 18–19 Denise
Kappa; 19r michael rubin; 21r Nicholas Rjabow; 20l Jenny Woodworth
www.ukemergency.co.uk
20–21

Words in **bold** can be found in the glossary on page 23.

Contents

What is a police car? 4

Lights and sirens 6

Police car equipment 8

High-speed cars 10

Special police cars 12

Police vans 14

Driving a police car 16

Police on two wheels 18

Land, air and sea............................... 20

Activities 22

Glossary 23

Index... 24

What is a police car?

A police car is an **emergency** vehicle driven by police officers. They use police cars to control **traffic**, **patrol** the streets and chase criminals.

Not all police cars are big and fast. This is an electric city patrol car.

Police cars are different from normal cars. They often have bigger engines, and better brakes and tyres.

Lights and sirens

Police cars have flashing lights and noisy sirens. Red-and-blue flashing lights warn other drivers that a police car is coming. Loud sirens make long screeching noises or blips.

Police cars have colourful blocks and stripes, so they can easily be seen.

Some of the markings on police cars are **reflective**, which makes them shine at night. The markings make the cars easy for people to recognize.

A police officer uses lights and sirens to make sure people can see and hear the car.

Police car
equipment

Police cars have lots of special equipment inside, including a **two-way radio**. Police officers use the radio to talk to other officers or the police headquarters.

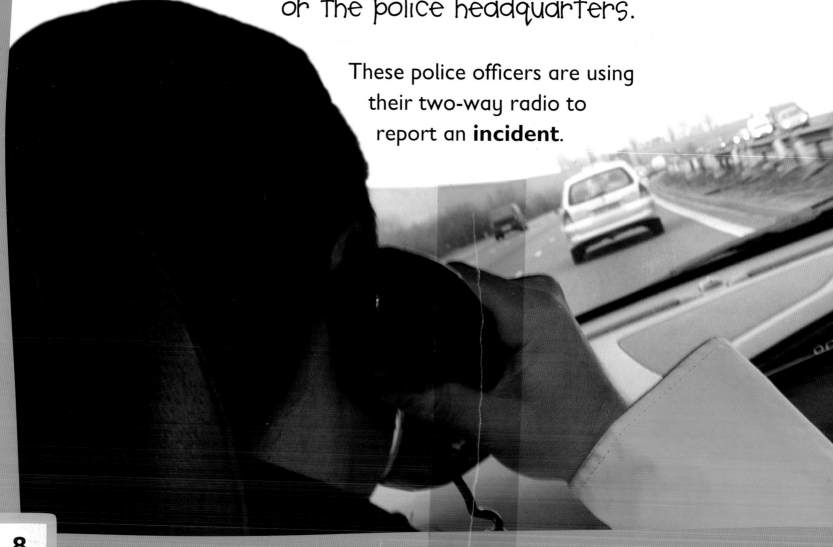

These police officers are using their two-way radio to report an **incident**.

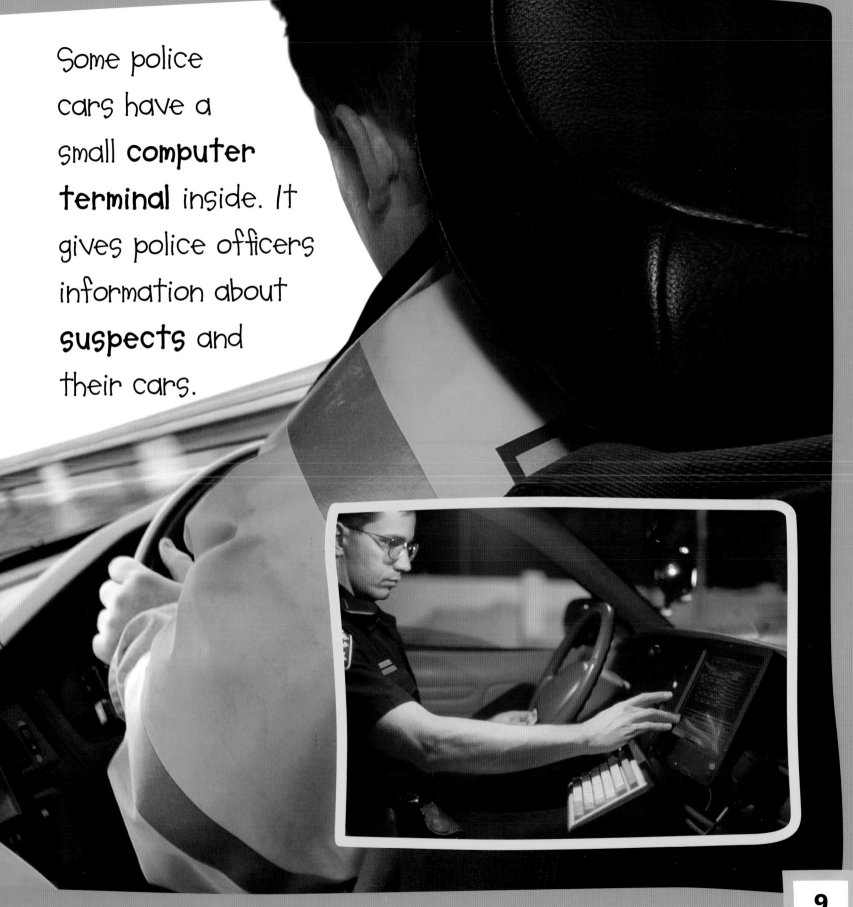

Some police cars have a small **computer terminal** inside. It gives police officers information about **suspects** and their cars.

High-speed cars

A pursuit car is a very fast police car. Police officers use them to chase criminals. Pursuit cars are normally powerful sports cars.

This Italian pursuit car is a Maserati sports car.

In the future, pursuit cars might look like this T1 supercar.

In the future, some police officers may use cars that are similar to racing cars. They will be able to reach speeds of nearly 200 miles an hour.

Special police cars

Police forces also have special-purpose cars. Some forces have rescue cars with **four-wheel drive** for going **off road**. They can be used to reach people on ground, such as sand, that normal cars cannot easily drive on.

EMERGENCY
CALL 9-1-1 FIRE POLICE MEDICAL

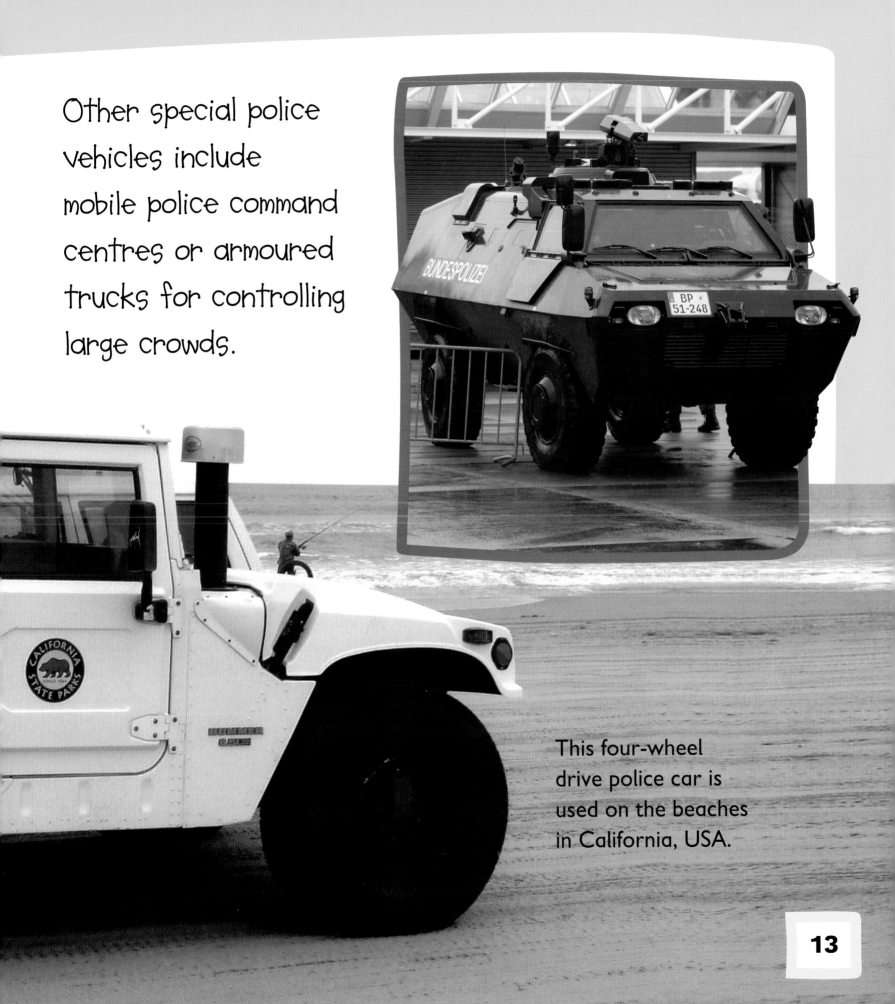

Other special police vehicles include mobile police command centres or armoured trucks for controlling large crowds.

This four-wheel drive police car is used on the beaches in California, USA.

Police vans

Police forces have vans for transporting people and equipment. Some police forces have teams of officers that deal with dangerous criminals who carry weapons. They travel in armoured vans.

This police van has a
windscreen protector.

Some vans are
used for taking
police officers and
suspects to where
they are needed.

An armoured van is
built in a special way,
so it is protected
against attack.

Driving a police car

Police officers have to drive fast when they are chasing suspects. This can be dangerous for the police officers and other drivers on the road, so they are specially trained to drive at high speeds.

Police officers must be able to control a car in any type of weather.

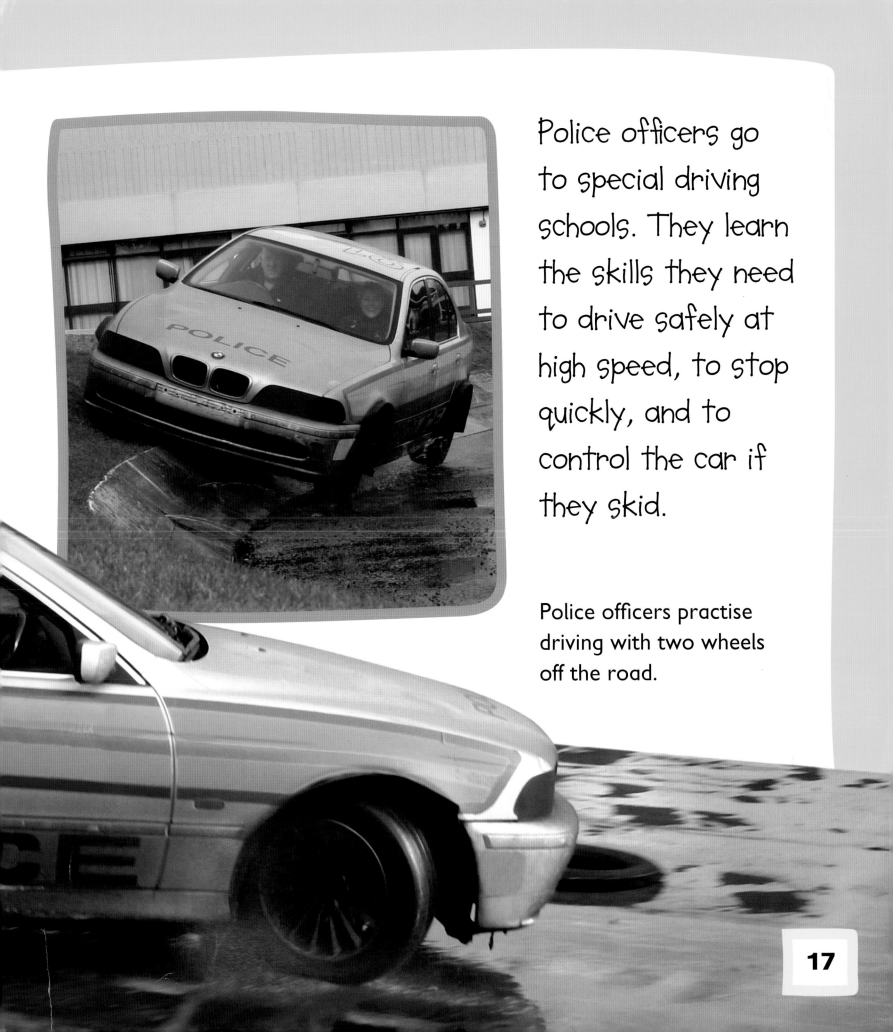

Police officers go to special driving schools. They learn the skills they need to drive safely at high speed, to stop quickly, and to control the car if they skid.

Police officers practise driving with two wheels off the road.

Police on two wheels

Police officers use motorcycles as well as cars. Motorcycles are good for moving through traffic in busy city streets. Traffic officers use them for patrolling motorways and for riding alongside cars transporting important people.

A highway, or motorway, patrol motorcycle in the USA.

Town and city police officers can travel more quickly by bicycle than on foot.

Land, air and sea

The police also use aircraft, horses and boats. Police use helicopters to follow criminals on the ground and to check for traffic jams. Police officers ride horses to patrol the streets.

Police officers are often seen on horseback in towns and cities.

Police use motorboats to patrol rivers and shorelines in cities. They can search suspicious boats and rescue people from the water.

Activities

- Which picture shows a police motorcycle, a pursuit car and a police boat?

- Make a drawing of your favourite police car. What sort of car is it? Does it have lights and sirens? What colour is it?

- Write a story about a police chase. It could be anywhere in the world – or even on another planet! What car would you drive? What crime would you be fighting? How dangerous would it be? How long would it take?

- Which of these police cars would be used to control a large crowd?

Glossary

Computer terminal
A machine that lets people look at information stored on a computer.

Emergency
A dangerous situation that must be dealt with straight away.

Four-wheel drive
Where all the wheels of a vehicle are turned by the engine.

Incident
Something that happens.

Off road
When a vehicle can be used on rough ground.

Patrol
To walk or drive around an area several times to check for trouble or danger.

Reflective
A material that light bounces off very well.

Siren
A machine that makes a loud, screeching noise.

Suspect
Someone who the police think is guilty of committing a crime.

Traffic
Cars, trucks, motorcycles and other vehicles on the road.

Two-way radio
A radio set that lets people talk to each other.

Index

aircraft 20
armoured vehicles 13, 14

bicycles 19
boats 20, 21

computers 9, 23
cutting machines 12

four-wheel drive 12, 13, 23

helicopters 20
highway patrols 18
horses 20

lights 6

mobile police command
centres 13
motorcycles 18

patrols 4, 18, 21, 23
police drivers 16, 17
police vans 14, 15
pursuit cars 10–11

radar guns 9, 23
rescue cars 12

sirens 6, 23
SWAT team 14

traffic control 4
traffic jams 20
traffic police 9, 11, 18
two-way radio 8, 9, 23

vans 14, 15